THE MINIATURE BOOK OF
Flower Arranging

MARY LAWRENCE

CRESCENT BOOKS
New York

This 1991 edition published by Crescent Books, distributed
by Outlet Book Company, Inc., a Random House Company,
225 Park Avenue South, New York, New York 10003, U.S.A.

© Salamander Books Ltd., 1991
129-137 York Way, London N7 9LG, United Kingdom

Printed and bound in Singapore

ISBN 0-517-03391-7
8 7 6 5 4 3 2

The publishers would like to thank Geest Plc. for supplying
the flowers used in this book.

CREDITS

MANAGING EDITOR: *Jilly Glassborow*
EDITED BY: *Veronica Ross*
PHOTOGRAPHY BY: *Richard Paines*
DESIGN AND ARTWORK BY: *Pauline Bayne*
TYPESET BY: *SX Composing Ltd.*
COLOR SEPARATION BY: *P&W Graphics, Pte. Ltd.*
Printed in Singapore by Star Standard Industries Pte. Ltd.

CONTENTS

INTRODUCTION

Flowers have been used for decorative purposes since time immemorial. Today, the craft has undergone something of a revival and now most people probably have a plant or a vase of flowers in their home. There is no great mystique attached to arranging flowers. A simple posy can look as stunning as a more lavish arrangement, and once you have mastered the basic techniques you can go on to design your own displays.

When selecting flowers, choose blooms with crisp foliage, strong stems and firm flower buds. Re-cut the stems when you get home, and give the flowers a long drink before transferring them to shallow water and a warm room. To preserve the life of your blooms, add a spoonful of sugar, an aspirin tablet or even lemonade to the water, or purchase preservatives from a florist.

You will need some pieces of basic equipment before you start. A pair of florists' scissors is a good investment and a sharp knife is helpful for cutting away foliage. Florists' foam will keep your display in position. It readily absorbs water and just needs to be soaked before using. For heavier stems crumple wire mesh inside the container. A pin-holder may also be useful when designing an arrangement using a limited number of flowers.

Flowers can transform the appearance of a room, so think carefully about your display. Consider harmony and balance, colour and shape before you begin. Choose blooms to complement your decor or to enhance the container. Use contrasting colours to add depth or toning colours for a coordinated display.

Flowers never fail to delight, and the displays featured in this book will inspire you to create your own colourful, fragrant designs.

$\mathcal{D}$UET FOR PEONIES

❧

20 pink peonies
3 bunches of blue cornflowers
6 sprays of eucalyptus
String & two jugs

$\mathcal{T}$he floral design on these pretty blue and pink patterned jugs is beautifully complemented by the choice of peonies and rich blue cornflowers for this elegant tied (hostess) bunch. Arrange a fan shape of eucalyptus foliage in the hand and secure with string. Bind the peonies firmly into the bunch following the shape of the foliage and adding in extra budding peonies, foliage and open peonies as you work. Add a flourish of cornflowers down one side and finish with a short bunch at the base of the display. Tie off the string and insert the arrangement into a jug. For the smaller jug display, cut down four peony stems so that the heads fall over the rim of the jug. To finish off, position the three cornflowers in the centre of the display.

$\mathcal{O}$VERTURE

15 yellow ranuculus
1 bunch yellow genista
5 orange tulips
3 blue irises
Ivy trails
Patterned jug

This bright and pretty cottage style display will be a welcome addition to any kitchen. The vivid colours on the floral patterned jug have been carefully picked out in the use of the fresh flowers. The narrow neck of the jug firmly grips the display and helps to secure the flowers in position.

Begin by arranging a posy of ranuculus in the hand. Clean and trim the stems and place them in the jug of water. Add an outline of genista and position the irises to give depth to the design. Insert the orange tulips at random throughout the arrangement to give an extra burst of colour. Finally tuck in wispy trails of ivy to spill over the rim of the jug and to add a final decorative touch to the design.

$\int$PRING CHORUS

〜

2 bunches of daffodils
Daffodil leaves
3 bunches of forget-me-nots
Woven basket
Wire mesh
Plastic container to fit basket

A wicker basket provides a perfect country setting for this charming display of spring daffodils and early forget-me-nots. Before starting your display, line the wicker basket with a plastic container to protect it and fill with crunched wire mesh.

Position one bunch of daffodils at the back of the container adding in the daffodil foliage to give a natural look. Group the forget-me-nots into several small bunches and insert throughout the basket with some tucked into the front so that they just peep over the edge. Cut down the stems of the remaining bunch of daffodils, and position them at random in among the forget-me-nots to complete this picturesque country setting.

$\mathcal{I}$RIS REPRISE

~

3 yellow irises
5 blue irises
Bunch of mixed narcissus
Bunch of primroses
Periwinkle flowers
Hazel catkins
Ivy foliage
Floral teapot
Wire mesh

$\mathcal{T}$he pretty floral pattern on this teapot has been cleverly picked out in the use of the blue and yellow iris. The bold outlines and strong colours of the iris complement the rich honeyed tones of the pine dresser.

Fill the teapot with crunched wire mesh. Position the iris so that they lean in the direction of the teapot spout, with the shortest stems in the centre of the pot to form the focal point. Intermingle the arrangement with the catkins and place the narcissi at random through the display. To finish, tuck in the periwinkle flowers, primroses and the ivy leaves.

ℰNSEMBLE

∽

5 moluccella (bells of Ireland)
5 white sweet peas
5 white freesia
3 white stock
1 white carnation
2 sprays green love-lies-bleeding
Collection of blue bottles

These pretty, old fashioned medicine bottles enhance the pure line of this cool summer display of
green and white flowers. This arrangment looks especially
attractive silhouetted against a pale background.

Insert the bells of Ireland into the tallest bottles at the
back of the arrangement to give the display height and a
sweeping background shape. Place the feathery sweet
peas in the smaller bottles at the front, along with the freesias and stocks. The solid white carnation adds depth to
the design. Position the soft sprays of love-lies-bleeding at
the very front to gently sweep down to meet the crisp white
tablecloth.

$\mathscr{P}$EACH QUINTET

15 peach floribunda roses
7 sprays of peach carnations
7 sprays pale peach carnations
Variegated ivy leaves
Posy bowl
Florists' foam

This charming, fresh looking posy of peach coloured roses combined with carnations looks very pleasing. The muted shades of the peach blooms match the decor of this room perfectly.

Fill the posy bowl with soaked florists' foam. Place ivy leaves around the edge so that they overlap a little. Cut a single rose bud stem to one and a third the height of the container and position in the centre of the bowl. Gradually add in the remaining roses while turning the bowl round to create an even effect. Use the open and budding carnations to fill in, placing the two shades of peach blooms at random throughout the arrangement, but taking care not to overlap the base leaves.

$\mathscr{P}$RELUDE

≈

20 cerise hyacinths
20 white daffodils
20 muscari
Serving dish
Wire mesh
Florist' foam
Water resistant tape

This elegant serving dish is a perfect container for a pyramid flower design and makes a superb decoration for a buffet table. Begin by forming the florists' foam into a cone shape and then wrap in wire mesh. Attach to the dish with water resistant tape, and soak well in water.

Position a hyacinth bud at the top of the cone, and slowly turning the dish towards you add in the remaining hyacinths graduating in size down towards the edge of the dish to create a pyramid shape. Tuck in the white daffodils between the sprays of hyacinths and finally add the blue muscari to define the shape and provide colour contrast.

$\mathcal{C}$OUNTRY REEL

∽

9 pink ranunculus
11 love-in-a-mist
3 sprays of pinks
Ivy foliage
Maple foliage
String
Jug

With a little time and care a simple bunch of garden flowers can be transformed into a charming hostess bunch fit to adorn any sitting room. These pink blooms mixed with green foliage look particularly pretty.

Separate the flowers and foliage into mixed groups. Cut each group to a different length and strip the lower leaves from the stems. Start by tying string to the tallest bunch of flowers and then tie in the smaller bunches, turning the bunch as you work. Place the most dominant colour at the base of the design. Make sure there is a balanced all round effect and break up any solid areas of colour or foliage by tying in single stems of foliage.

$\mathcal{B}$UTTERFLY

Several small branches of apple blossom
5 pink tulips
Chinese bowl
Large metal pinholder
Florists' foam

The natural simplicity and freshness of flowering apple blossom combined with pale pink tulips adds a timeless tranquility to this oriental setting. The chinese bowl gives the display an authentic look.

Use a large metal pinholder in the bottom of the bowl to act as a balance and fill with well soaked florists' foam. Strip the bark from the lower stems of the apple branches and crush the stems with a hammer to aid drinking. Position two branches at the back of the bowl at an oblique angle. Place the shorter branches at the front of the bowl at the same angle. Add the final branch of blossom and position it so that it bends down to touch the table. Starting from the left, and following the line of the final branch, position the tulips to make a central focal point.

TEA FOR TWO

20 white ranunculus
Sprays of hedge parsley
Ivy foliage
Green plastic covered florists' mesh
Green glass dish
Florists' tape

In the early stages of flowering, white ranunculus have a greenish tinge which combines beautifully with the sprays of hedge parsley and ivy to make this charming display a welcome addition to your afternoon tea table.

Secure the crushed mesh into the glass dish with florists' tape. Cut one ranunculus stem to two and a half times the height of the sundae dish and position in the centre of the display. Surround the central stem with the remaining ranunculus which cascade down and over the edge of the dish. Add ivy leaves among the blooms to give crispness and depth to the design, and fill in with the sprays of hedge parsley and the remaining ranunculus buds.

CONCERTO

11 pink antirrhinums
13 pink carnations
5 pink zinnias
7 sprays of peach carnations
2 bunches of deep pink sweet peas
5 scabious (pincushion flower)
7 agapanthus
Sprays of sprengeri fern
Crystal vase
Wire mesh
Florists' tape

This stunning display of predominately pink flowers looks surprisingly pretty against a vivid pink floral background. To start bend a circle of wire mesh over the top of the vase and secure in position with tape. Build up a fan-shaped outline with the antirrhinum, sweet pea and spray carnation. Position the large pink carnations to create a focal point and arrange sweet pea and fern to spill over the front of the vase. Use zinnias, scabious and aga-panthus to give depth and added colour to the display.

$\mathcal{C}$ARMEN

6 stems red gladioli
7 stems bells of Ireland
Marguerites
Rectangular glass container
Medium sized piece of charcoal

$\mathcal{T}$he simple rectangular glass container used here complements the dramatic quality of the gladioli and continues the line of the design under water adding a pleasing contrast to the blaze of colour.

Fill the container three-quarters full with water. Clean all the flower stems as they will be visible under water. Cut one gladioli stem to three times the height of the container and position so that it leans to the left at the back. Trim five gladioli so that they graduate downwards in size and position them along the back of the vase with bells of Ireland placed in between. Cut short the remaining gladioli and place at the front right edge. Use the marguerites to fill the front of the display. Wedge the charcoal at the back of the vase to keep the water clear.

HARMONY

12 stems of mauve freesias
12 mauve roses
10 mauve sweet peas
20 purple anemones
Ivy foliage
Eucalyptus foliage
Silver dish
Glass bowl
Florists' foam and florists' tape

The beautiful floral fretwork on this silver dish looks stunning against the dark wood of the dining table and harmonizes well with the mauve and purple blooms used for this informal table arrangement.

Place a glass bowl filled with foam inside the silver dish and secure with florists' tape. Place the foliages around the edge of the dish allowing the ivy to trail onto the table. Insert a rose in the centre of the bowl and position the remaining roses to graduate down to the edge. Add the sweet peas, freesias and dark anemones among the roses.

ORCHESTRATION

12 stems of delphinium
18 yellow antirrhinums
5 heads of blue/mauve hydrangeas
Large vase
Wire mesh
Florists' securing tape

Choose a tall sturdy vase and bold elegant flowers to create this stunning floor standing arrangement, which will complement any sitting room or hallway. Loosely pack the vase with crumpled wire mesh. Bend a circle of wire mesh to overlap the rim of the vase and secure in position with florists' tape. Fill with water.

Place the tallest delphinium stem in the centre of the vase. Position the other delphiniums in front and to the side of the central stem, graduating downwards in height to create an even effect. Intersperse the delphiniums with yellow antirrhinum following the line of the design, and to complete the arrangement place the hydrangea blooms around the neck of the vase.

SYMPHONY

7 stems of delphinium
7 pink peonies & 9 pale pink roses
6 white antirrhinum
4 stems of bells of Ireland
3 stems of green love-lies-bleeding
3 sprays of pink alstroemeria
5 stems of astrantia
Oval Victorian tureen
Wire mesh & string

This stunning display captures all the beauty and freshness of a summer garden. Crunch a piece of wire mesh into the tureen and secure with string. Build up height in the centre of the display with a single tall delphinium stem. Place the remaining delphiniums, the bells of Ireland and antirrhinum around the central stem so that they curve gracefully towards the table. Place three peonies in the centre to give depth to the design and fill in with the single blooms of roses and peonies. Position alstroemeria and astrantia to soften the outline.

ORCHID SONATA

6 sprays of striped & red arachnis orchids
2 sprays of white orchids
1 spray of red & white dendrobium
Red leaved foliage 'smoke tree' (Cotinus Coggygria)
Small brass watering can
Florists' foam

These readily available and lasting orchids have a fascinating and distinctive beauty of their own and this simple arrangement emphasizes the detail of each individual bloom.

Pack soaked florists' foam into a decorative miniature brass watering can. Place the red and striped arachnis orchids at the back of the container following the slope of the spout. Trim the buds from some of the white orchids and place them to the front right of the arrangement to follow the line through to the top of the spout. Place the dendrobium orchids in the centre of the arrangement and fill in with small sprays of red foliage.

$\mathcal{R}$HAPSODY

11 red antirrhinums
7 red peonies
5 sweet Williams
6 white stocks
1 bunch red sweet peas
White poplar foliage
Large decorative jug & wire mesh

The striking display of vivid red and pure white flowers beautifully complements the attractive floral pattern on the vase. Begin by crunching the wire mesh securely into the jug. Cut down one antirrhinum stem to twice the height of the jug and position it at the centre back of the jug.

Arrange the remaining antirrhinum around the curve of the jug and intermingle the poplar foliage. Place a swathe of peonies from back to centre and repeat using sweet peas. The white stocks introduce pleasing colour contrast throughout the centre of the design. Fill in with sweet William and poplar foliage to spill over the rim of the jug.

$\mathcal{C}$HRISTMAS CAROL

22 red carnations & 20 red spray carnations
7 bells of Ireland & 7 green love-lies-bleeding
10 red alstroemeria & 7 auratum lilies
10 sprays red arachnis orchids
Branches of tortured willow
Gold ribbon 4ins (10cms) wide & gold spray paint
Large heavy oval container
2 small heavy oval containers
Ivy, ruscus & pine foliage
Florists' foam & waterproof tape

$\mathcal{F}$ill the containers with soaked florists' foam and
secure with tape. Spray the lillies and willow
branches with gold paint. Form the ruscus into a fan
shaped outline in the central container. Build-up the
shape with mixed red flowers using the gold lilies as a
central line. Place a gold bow at the centre base of the container so it trails over the mantelpiece. Add in the sprays
of ruscus. Position the willow in the side containers and
intersperse with sprays of orchids. Cover the base with
pine foliage. Finish off by adding in remaining gold lilies.